Autism & PDD™
Expanding
Social Options

Pam Britton Reese
Nena C. Challenner

Skill Area:	social skills
Ages:	6 thru 18
Grades:	1 thru 12

LinguiSystems, Inc.
3100 4th Avenue
East Moline, IL 61244-9700
1-800 PRO IDEA
1-800-776-4332

FAX: 1-800-577-4555
E-mail: service@linguisystems.com
Web: www.linguisystems.com
TDD: 1-800-933-8331
             (for those with hearing impairments)

Copyright © 2003 LinguiSystems, Inc.

All of our products are copyrighted to protect the fine work of our authors. You may only copy the student materials as needed for your own use with students. Any other reproduction or distribution of the pages in this book is prohibited, including copying the entire book to use as another primary source or "master" copy.

Printed in the U.S.A.

ISBN 0-7606-0499-1

About the Authors

Pam Britton Reese, M.A., CCC-SLP, is a speech-language pathologist with over eight years experience working with children with autism. She is currently enrolled in the Ph.D program at the University of Texas at Dallas. While there, she is helping to launch a class for preschool children exhibiting problems with social communication and social relationships. Pam is also the author of *The Source for Alzheimers & Dementia*.

Nena C. Challenner, M.Ed., is an assistant principal at Long-branch Elementary School in Midlothian, Texas. She has over 20 years of experience in general and special education.

Pam and Nena have also written *Autism & PDD: Social Skills Lessons* (Primary, Intermediate, Adolescent), *Autism & PDD: Safety*, and *Autism & PDD: Basic Reading Comprehension Kit*.

Edited by Lauri Whiskeyman
Illustrations by Eulala Conner and Ken Prestley
Page Layout by Christine Buysse
Cover Design by Mike Paustian

Table of Contents

Introduction

When we wrote our series of books: *Autism & PDD: Social Skills Lessons* (Primary, Intermediate, and Adolescent), we often thought that we needed to give more than one (or two) options for how to do something socially. Too often, a child with autism will learn a response to a social situation and use only that response every time. This leaves the child with autism with a limited social repertoire which severely restricts his or her social interactions.

In *Exiting Nirvana: A Daughter's Life with Autism* (2001), Clara Claiborne Park discusses the social contract she would make with her daughter, Jessy. "Jessy had no idea what I meant when I included such items as 'Saying Something Interesting' or 'Doing Something to Help'" (p. 162). She described how she would work with Jessy to come up with six specific behaviors for each social situation. Over time, Clara observed Jessy using the social behaviors appropriately in different settings and at times adding examples of her own.

Choices are important in the lives of people with autism. In the *Autism & PDD: Social Skills Lessons* books (Intermediate and Adolescent), we used Choice Sheets (e.g., *Anger* and *When People Bother Me*). These Choice Sheets were effective with the students and we saw a way to build in all the social options we had wanted to use while teaching children about social situations. *Autism & PDD: Expanding Social Options* is the next step after social skills lessons for students to learn about social situations. Social skills lessons help students understand the "why" of what they need to do. Social options give them multiple forms of "how" to do it.

Autism & PDD: Expanding Social Options contains social situations that many children face. For each situation, we have listed five or six options. The social situations teach social communication (e.g., "Here are some ways I can greet people.") and social self control (e.g., "Here are some things I can do when it is too noisy.").

Introduce the social situations one at a time. Choose the situations that are most relevant for each child. Practicing the situations with role play is also helpful. The tracking forms on pages 65-69 can be used for documentation. The tracking form for individuals can be used to take notes on how a particular child does on the lessons. The tracking form for groups can be used to keep track of group participation.

We think that social options offer flexibility in many social situations and in addition, provide a scaffold to organize social information. We have only suggested a few options for each social category, but certainly, more could be added. Like Jessy, children with autism may learn to observe and discover other options after practicing and becoming familiar with the options presented in this book.

Pam and Nena

Here are some ways I can greet people:

Wave one hand.

Say, "Hi."

Say, "Hello."

Say, "Hi _____."
(person's name)

Say, "How are you?"

Say, "It's good to see you."

Here are some ways I can ask for help:

 Touch someone's arm and say, "Help."

 Say, "Help."

 Say, "Will you help me?"

 Say, "Please help me."

 Say, "I need help."

 Say how I need help: _____

Here are some ways I can say "Good-bye":

Wave one hand.

Say, "Good-bye."

Say, "Bye."

Say, "See you later."

Say, "So long!"

Say, "Gotta go now!"

Social Communication
Expanding Social Options

9

Copyright © 2003 LinguiSystems, Inc.

Here are some ways I can get someone's attention:

 Touch someone's arm.

 Touch someone's shoulder.

 Look in someone's eyes.

 Say, "Excuse me."

 Raise my hand.

 Wave my hand.

Here are some ways I can say "I'm sorry":

Say, "I'm sorry."

Say, "Sorry."

Say, "I didn't mean to."

Say, "I won't do it again."

Give a hug.

Copyright © 2003 LinguiSystems, Inc.

Here are some ways I can meet a new person:

Say, "Hi, what's your name?"

Say, "My name is _____."

Say, "I'm _____."

(name)

Say, "It's nice to meet you."

Shake hands.

Copyright © 2003 LinguiSystems, Inc.

Here are some things I can do if someone says something nice to me:

 Say, "Thank you."

 Look at the person and smile.

 Say, "That's nice!"

 Say, "That makes me happy!"

 Say, "You're very nice."

Copyright © 2003 LinguiSystems, Inc.

Here are some nice things I can say to people:

Say, "You look nice today."

Say, "I like your _____."

Say, "You're nice."

Say, "You are good at _____."

Say, "I like you."

Social Communication
Expanding Social Options   14   Copyright © 2003 LinguiSystems, Inc.

Here are some ways I can say "No":

Say, "No."

Shake my head.

Say, "I don't want to _____."

Say, "I can't."

Walk away.

Here are some ways I can thank people:

 Say, "Thank you."

 Say, "Thanks a lot!"

 Smile.

 Say, "I appreciate that."

 Give a hug.

 Write a thank-you note.

Here are some ways I can join a group of people talking:

 Stand close to the people.

 Look at the people talking.

 Touch a person one time on the elbow or shoulder.

 Say, "Hi!"

 Say, "Guess what?"

 Say, "_____."

Here are some ways I can stop talking with people:

 Say, "I need to go now."

 Say, "See you later."

 Say, "Nice to talk with you."

 Wave one hand.

 Take one step backward.

 Leave.

Here are some things I can talk to people about:

school

the weather

a recent holiday

my family

something in the news

something personal
(Examples: new baby, new pet, haircut)

Here are some ways I can help at home:

Take out the garbage.

Load the dishwasher.

Set the table.

Sweep the floor.

Vacuum the rug.

Dust the furniture.

Here are some ways I can help a friend:

 Carry something.

 Hold the door open.

 Look for something lost.

 Share things.

 Pick up something a friend dropped.

 Listen to a friend.

Here are some ways to say "I don't know":

Say, "I don't know."

Say, "I'm not sure."

Say, "I need help."

Say, "I can't remember."

Say, "I don't know the answer."

Here are some ways I can ask a friend to play:

 Say, "Want to play?"

 Say, "Let's _____."
(game/activity)

 Say, "Want to do something?"

 Say, "Come on, let's play."

 Say, "Let's go outside."

Here are some ways I can show love to people:

   Give a hug.

   Give a kiss on the cheek.

   Pat the person's back.

   Hold a hand.

   Give a present.

   Make a card.

Here are some ways I can be nice to a friend:

Call my friend on the phone.

Smile.

Ask my friend to play.

Give my friend a present.

Say, "Hi" when I see my friend.

Sit together on the bus or in the lunchroom.

Here are some ways I can volunteer to help:

 Raise my hand.

 Say, "I can help."

 Say, "Let me."

 Say, "I know how to do that."

 Say, "I will."

Here are some things I can say when I don't understand:

 Say, "I don't understand."

 Say, "Will you repeat that?"

 Say, "I don't get it."

 Say, "Will you explain that?"

 Say, "Show me what you mean."

Copyright © 2003 LinguiSystems, Inc.

Here are some things I can do when someone is crying:

 Give the person a tissue.

 Pat the person on the back.

 Give the person a hug.

 Say, "Are you okay?"

 Sit next to the person.

 Try to make the person laugh.

Here are some ways I can disagree:

 Say, "I don't agree with that."

 Say, "I don't believe so."

 Say, "I don't think that is right."

 Shake my head "No."

 Say, "No."

Social Communication
Expanding Social Options

29

Copyright © 2003 LinguiSystems, Inc.

Here are some things I can do when someone breaks a rule:

Tell the person the rule.

Walk away.

Say, "Don't do that."

Say, "You are breaking a rule."

Tell an adult.

Copyright © 2003 LinguiSystems, Inc.

Here are some ways I can interrupt a person:

Say, "Excuse me."

Tap the person on the shoulder one time.

Say, "May I interrupt?"

Say, "I'm sorry to interrupt."

Say, "Pardon me."

Stand by the person and look at him or her.

Copyright © 2003 LinguiSystems, Inc.

Here are some things I can do when I am bored:

Look at a book.

Take a walk.

Watch TV.

Listen to music.

Draw.

Write.

Here are some things I can do when I am lonely:

Look at a photo album.

Talk to someone.

Write a letter.

Call someone.

Play with a pet.

Copyright © 2003 LinguiSystems, Inc.

Here are some things I can do when I am tired:

 Say, "Can I take a break?"

 Put my head down.

 Close my eyes and count to ten.

 Lie on the couch.

 Take a nap.

 Listen to music.

Here are some things I can do when I am hungry:

 Have something to drink.

 Say, "Is it time for lunch?"

 Ask for a snack.

 Eat a few crackers.

 Make something to eat.

Here are some things I can do in the car:

Look out the window.

Listen to the radio.

Look at a book.

Sing a song.

Sleep.

Talk to other people in the car.

Copyright © 2003 LinguiSystems, Inc.

Here are some things I can do when I get home from school:

Eat a snack.

Do my homework.

Play outside.

Play with toys.

Do a chore.

Watch TV.

Copyright © 2003 LinguiSystems, Inc.

Here are some things I can do with a dog:

 Feed the dog.

 Give the dog water.

 Pet the dog.

 Take the dog for a walk.

 Brush the dog.

 Play with the dog.

Here are some things I can do with a cat:

 Feed the cat.

 Give the cat water.

 Pet the cat.

 Hold the cat.

 Listen to the cat purr.

 Play with the cat.

Copyright © 2003 LinguiSystems, Inc.

Here are some things I can do with my brother/sister:

Play a board game.

Watch TV.

Look at a book.

Work a puzzle.

Play outside.

Play with toys.

Here are some things I can do at the doctor's office:

Look at a magazine.

Read my book.

Talk to Mom or Dad.

Draw.

Play with toys.

Wait quietly.

Here are some things I can do at a library:

Choose a book.

Listen to a story.

Look at a magazine.

Use the computer.

Sit and read a book.

Copyright © 2003 LinguiSystems, Inc.

Here are some things I can do at a grocery store:

 Help push the cart.

 Read the shopping list.

 Help find the food.

 Put food in the cart.

 Cross things off the shopping list.

Copyright © 2003 LinguiSystems, Inc.

Here are some things I can do at a playground:

Go on the slide.

Swing.

Climb.

Run.

Dig in the sand.

Watch the other people.

Here are some things I can say when I don't want food:

Say, "No, thanks."

Say, "I'm not hungry."

Say, "Thanks, I don't want any."

Say, "I don't like that."

Say, "I don't care for any."

Copyright © 2003 LinguiSystems, Inc.

Here are some things I can say when I get a present:

Say, "What a surprise!"

Say, "Can I open it now?"

Say, "This is great!"

Say, "Thank you!"

Say "That was nice of you."

Here are some things I can do when someone corrects me:

 Stop and listen.

 Say, "Okay."

 Say, "I didn't know."

 Say, "Thank you for telling me."

 Say, "Is this right?"

Here are some things I can do while I wait:

 Look at a book.

 Look out the window.

 Think about _____.

 Play with my _____.

 Cross my arms.

Here are some things to say when I am upset:

Say, "I'm mad."

Say, "I'm worried about _____."

Say, "Please stop."

Say, "I don't want to talk right now."

Say, "I need a break."

Here are some things I can do if something is bothering me:

 Tell an adult.

 Walk away.

 Say, "Please stop."

 Say, "Leave me alone."

 Say, "Don't do that!"

Here are some things I can do to relax:

Listen to music.

Look at a book.

Close my eyes.

Squeeze a pillow.

Take a bath or shower.

Watch TV.

Here are some things I can do when it is too noisy:

Leave the room.

Say, "That's too loud."

Wear earplugs.

Wear headphones.

Say, "Please be quiet."

Cover my ears.

Here are some things I can do if I feel sick:

 Tell an adult.

 Lie down.

 Go to the clinic at school.

 Get a drink of water.

 Say, "My _____ hurts."

Copyright © 2003 LinguiSystems, Inc.

Here are some things I can do if I want to be alone:

 Say, "I don't want to talk right now."

 Go to my room.

 Say, "I want to be alone."

 Say, "Can we talk later?"

 Read a book.

 Go outside.

Copyright © 2003 LinguiSystems, Inc.

Here are some things I can do when someone is mean to me:

 Walk away.

 Tell an adult.

 Say, "Stop it."

 Say, "I don't like that."

 Find another friend.

Copyright © 2003 LinguiSystems, Inc.

Here are some things I can do when I feel angry:

 Say, "I'm mad."

 Take a walk.

 Go to a quiet area.

 Listen to music.

 Take deep breaths.

Self-Control
Expanding Social Options   56   Copyright © 2003 LinguiSystems, Inc.

Here are some things I can do when I feel sad:

 Say, "I'm sad."

 Talk to a friend.

 Go to a quiet place.

 Cry a little.

 Listen to music.

Here are some things I can do when I feel afraid:

Say, "I'm afraid."

Tell an adult.

Say, "That scares me."

Ask for a hug.

Walk away.

Copyright © 2003 LinguiSystems, Inc.

Here are some things I can do when I feel happy:

 Smile.

 Laugh.

 Clap my hands.

 Give a hug.

 Say, "I'm happy."

 Sing.

Here are some things I can do when I feel disappointed:

 Say, "I'm disappointed."

 Say, "Maybe next time."

 Say, "I'll try again."

 Say, "That's okay."

 Talk to a friend.

Copyright © 2003 LinguiSystems, Inc.

Here are some things I can do when I feel excited:

 Clap my hands.

 Laugh.

 Give a high five.

 Say, "I'm excited."

 Say, "Yea!"

Self-Control
Expanding Social Options
61
Copyright © 2003 LinguiSystems, Inc.

Here are some things I can do when I feel frustrated:

 Say, "I feel frustrated."

 Say, "I need help."

 Take a break.

 Take deep breaths.

 Take a walk.

Copyright © 2003 LinguiSystems, Inc.

Here are some things I can do if I am hurt:

Find an adult.

Say, "Help."

Say, "Ouch."

Say, "I'm hurt."

Say, "I hurt my _____."

Go to the clinic at school.

Here are some things I can do if someone is bothering my toys:

 Say, "Stop."

 Say, "I want to play with it myself."

 Say, "Find another toy."

 Say, "Please don't touch my toy."

 Say, "You can have it next."

 Tell an adult.

Copyright © 2003 LinguiSystems, Inc.

Tracking Form for Lessons–Individual

Name _____

Social Communication

❒ Greet people
Date _____
_____
_____

❒ Ask for help
Date _____
_____
_____

❒ Say "Good-bye"
Date _____
_____
_____

❒ Get someone's attention
Date _____
_____
_____

❒ Say "I'm sorry"
Date _____
_____
_____

❒ Meet a new person
Date _____
_____
_____

❒ If someone says something nice to me
Date _____
_____
_____

❒ Nice things to say to people
Date _____
_____
_____

❒ Say "No"
Date _____
_____
_____

❒ Thank people
Date _____
_____
_____

❒ Join a group of people talking
Date _____
_____
_____

❒ Stop talking with people
Date _____
_____
_____

❒ Things to talk to people about
Date _____
_____
_____

❒ Help at home
Date _____
_____
_____

❒ Help a friend
Date _____
_____
_____

❒ Say "I don't know"
Date _____
_____
_____

❒ Ask a friend to play
Date _____
_____
_____

❒ Show love to people
Date _____
_____
_____

❒ Be nice to a friend
Date _____
_____
_____

❒ Volunteer to help
Date _____
_____
_____

Tracking Form for Lessons–Individual

Name _____

Social Communication, *continued*

❑ When I don't understand
Date _____
_____
_____

❑ When someone is crying
Date _____
_____
_____

❑ Disagree
Date _____
_____
_____

❑ When someone breaks a rule
Date _____
_____
_____

❑ Interrupt a person
Date _____
_____
_____

❑ When I am bored
Date _____
_____
_____

❑ When I am lonely
Date _____
_____
_____

❑ When I am tired
Date _____
_____
_____

❑ When I am hungry
Date _____
_____
_____

❑ In the car
Date _____
_____
_____

❑ When I get home from school
Date _____
_____
_____

❑ With a dog
Date _____
_____
_____

❑ With a cat
Date _____
_____
_____

❑ With my brother/sister
Date _____
_____
_____

❑ At the doctor's office
Date _____
_____
_____

❑ At a library
Date _____
_____
_____

❑ At a grocery store
Date _____
_____
_____

❑ At a playground
Date _____
_____
_____

❑ When I don't want food
Date _____
_____
_____

❑ When I get a present
Date _____
_____
_____

Tracking Form for Lessons—Individual

Name _____

Self-Control

❏ When someone corrects me
Date _____
_____
_____

❏ While I wait
Date _____
_____
_____

❏ When I am upset
Date _____
_____
_____

❏ If something is bothering me
Date _____
_____
_____

❏ To relax
Date _____
_____
_____

❏ When it is too noisy
Date _____
_____
_____

❏ If I feel sick
Date _____
_____
_____

❏ If I want to be alone
Date _____
_____
_____

❏ When someone is mean to me
Date _____
_____
_____

❏ When I feel angry
Date _____
_____
_____

❏ When I feel sad
Date _____
_____
_____

❏ When I feel afraid
Date _____
_____
_____

❏ When I feel happy
Date _____
_____
_____

❏ When I feel disappointed
Date _____
_____
_____

❏ When I feel excited
Date _____
_____
_____

❏ When I feel frustrated
Date _____
_____
_____

❏ If I am hurt
Date _____
_____
_____

❏ If someone is bothering my toys
Date _____
_____
_____

Copyright © 2003 LinguiSystems, Inc.

Tracking Form for Lessons—Group

Names:					
Social Communication					
Greet people					
Ask for help					
Say "Good-bye"					
Get someone's attention					
Say "I'm sorry"					
Meet a new person					
If someone says something nice to me					
Nice things to say to people					
Say "No"					
Thank people					
Join a group of people talking					
Stop talking with people					
Things to talk to people about					
Help at home					
Help a friend					
Say "I don't know"					
Ask a friend to play					
Show love to people					
Be nice to a friend					
Volunteer to help					
When I don't understand					
When someone is crying					
Disagree					
When someone breaks a rule					
Interrupt a person					
When I am bored					
When I am lonely					
When I am tired					
When I am hungry					
In the car					
When I get home from school					

Tracking Form for Lessons–Group

Names:					
Social Communication, *continued*					
With a dog					
With a cat					
With my brother/sister					
At the doctor's office					
At a library					
At a grocery store					
At a playground					
When I don't want food					
When I get a present					
Self-Control					
When someone corrects me					
While I wait					
When I am upset					
If something is bothering me					
To relax					
When it is too noisy					
If I feel sick					
If I want to be alone					
When someone is mean to me					
When I feel angry					
When I feel sad					
When I feel afraid					
When I feel happy					
When I feel disappointed					
When I feel excited					
When I feel frustrated					
If I am hurt					
If someone is bothering my toys					

References

Park, C.C. *Exiting Nirvana: A Daughter's Life with Autism.* Boston: Little, Brown and Company, 2001.

Reese, P.B. and Challenner, N.C. *Autism and PDD: Adolescent Social Skills Lessons.* East Moline, IL: LinguiSystems, Inc., 2001.

Reese, P.B. and Challenner, N.C. *Autism and PDD: Intermediate Social Skills Lessons.* East Moline, IL: LinguiSystems, Inc., 2002.

Reese, P.B. and Challenner, N.C. *Autism and PDD: Primary Social Skills Lessons.* East Moline, IL: LinguiSystems, Inc., 1999.

19-05-987654

Copyright © 2003 LinguiSystems, Inc.